COLONIAL PEOPLE

The Colonial Minuteman

LAURA L. SULLIVAN

Cavendish
Square

New York

Published in 2016 by Cavendish Square Publishing, LLC
243 5th Avenue, Suite 136, New York, NY 10016

Copyright © 2016 by Cavendish Square Publishing, LLC

First Edition

Website: cavendishsq.com

This publication represents the opinions and views of the author based on his or her personal experience, knowledge, and research. The information in this book serves as a general guide only. The author and publisher have used their best efforts in preparing this book and disclaim liability rising directly or indirectly from the use and application of this book.

CPSIA Compliance Information: Batch #WS15CSQ

All websites were available and accurate when this book was sent to press.

Library of Congress Cataloging-in-Publication Data

Sullivan, Laura L., 1974-
The colonial Minuteman / Laura L. Sullivan.
pages cm. — (Colonial people)
Includes index.
ISBN 978-1-50260-478-1 (hardcover) ISBN 978-1-50260-479-8 (ebook)
1. Minutemen (Militia)—Juvenile literature. 2. United States—History—Revolution, 1775-1783—Juvenile literature.
3. Minutemen (Militia)—Massachusetts—Juvenile literature.
4. Massachusetts—History—Revolution, 1775-1783—Juvenile literature. I. Title.
E255.S85 2015
973.3—dc23
2014046811

Editorial Director: David McNamara
Editor: Andrew Coddington
Copy Editor: Cynthia Roby
Art Director: Jeffrey Talbot
Designer: Stephanie Flecha
Senior Production Manager: Jennifer Ryder-Talbot
Production Editor: Renni Johnson
Photo Research: J8 Media

Printed in the United States of America

CONTENTS

ONE

The Minutemen and Militias

The **minutemen** of Colonial America before and during the Revolutionary War were part of a long tradition of **militia** stretching back to the mother country of England. A militia is a military force made up not of professional soldiers, but rather ordinary citizens. Most of the time, they would live like regular **civilians**. Occasionally they would train for battle. In times of need, these men could be **mustered**, or called up, to fight.

In the Anglo-Saxon common law system in England, as far back as the fifth century CE, two traditions allowed for common citizens without any particular military training to be called for service. One, called the *posse comitatus* (Latin for "power of the community"), was organized by a sheriff or other law enforcement official to hunt

The minuteman, known for his ability to be ready for a fight at a minute's notice, became a symbol of American liberty.

down a wanted criminal. The word "posse" would later be widely used in the American Wild West when people banded together to hunt outlaws.

The other kind of civilian call-up in Anglo Saxon times was called the *fyrd*. All men, even noblemen, of each particular shire or county were obligated to take up arms when needed. They might have to help prevent civil unrest within their own area. Or more likely, they would have to respond to the main threat of the time: Viking raiding parties.

The English Militia Grows

The obligation to be part of a militia continued throughout English history. By the sixteenth century, the militia of England was well organized—but badly trained. Each region had to provide not only a list of eligible men for possible muster, but also an inventory of any weapons, armor, or horses people owned that could be used in times of crisis. They even kept a record of how much money people had, so they could force them to buy their own weapons if necessary. On paper, it looked very efficient. However, the militia rarely met and almost never trained.

The nation's leaders began to worry that they wouldn't be prepared for real trouble. So in the seventeenth century they organized several

Civilian militia, such as these reenactors pictured, fought on the side of Parliament in the English Civil War of 1642–1651.

elite militia forces. These were mostly centered in the city of London. The special militias met for frequent training, and became very skilled. Some took part in the English Civil War. All this time, the main military force still consisted of professional soldiers who did that as their primary job. Militias were the backup force.

American Colonies Build a Militia

When England began establishing **colonies** in the New World, the earliest settlers saw the need to continue the tradition of forming militias. England was too far away to provide soldiers quickly in case of emergency. Colonists were in danger from some Native American tribes, or from settlers of other nations such as France who wanted to expand into territory the British had claimed. Though the term minuteman is generally applied to the specialized militia active immediately before and during the American Revolutionary War, the history of the minuteman concept goes back much farther.

In the 1630s, about twenty thousand British citizens crossed the Atlantic to join the Massachusetts Bay Colony. All men of sound body between the ages of sixteen and sixty had to join the militia. The militia's first operation in America was less than spectacular. During the Pequot War in 1636, the Massachusetts Bay militia was sent to retaliate against a tribe after a local trader was killed. Unfortunately, no one seemed to know exactly which tribe was responsible. The militia marched on a village (possibly the wrong one) and destroyed it, but didn't kill any Native Americans. Then they marched home again. This uncoordinated response led to increased hostility against the settlers by various tribes.

The Minutemen

The four colonies then in existence (Plymouth, Connecticut, New Haven, and Massachusetts Bay) joined in the New England Confederation and decided to reorganize the militia. By 1645, a select group of the best militia members were chosen to be part of a rapid-deployment team. These were all men under thirty years old, with some natural ability and a strong enthusiasm to improve. The idea was that these men could be ready to fight at a minute's notice—hence the term minuteman. About 30 percent of the militia was made up of minutemen.

The minutemen and other militia members were also of vital importance during the series of conflicts collectively known as the French and Indian War. These conflicts were about who would control the North American interior. The common threat of the French and their allied tribes caused the colonies to unify. The final overwhelming defeat of the French by the British ultimately led to the conflict for which minutemen are best known: the American Revolutionary War. With the big threat of the French gone once and for all, the colonists didn't have such a need for the support and protection of their homeland.

The Minutemen at Lexington and Concord

The opening **salvo** of the Revolutionary War took place on April 19, 1775, in what came to be known as the Battles of Lexington and Concord. Colonists were angry over what they considered to be unfair **taxation** by England, among other issues. Rebellion was brewing. British authorities in Boston, alarmed by the swelling numbers of militia, sent a secret force to Concord to take control of the weapons and supplies there. But colonists caught wind of the scheme.

On the night of April 18, minuteman Paul Revere made his famous "Midnight Ride" to alert the militia that the British army was coming. The militia in Lexington was outnumbered, and the British managed to pass through, but the minutemen mustered so quickly at Concord that the English troops were forced to retreat back to Boston. The minutemen and other militia members followed them all the way, firing on the columns of soldiers. On the British side, 73 were killed, 174 were wounded, and 26 were missing. On the colonial side, 49 were killed and 39 were wounded (though this includes not just minutemen but also civilians who spontaneously fought in the towns along the route of the Army's retreat).

Throughout the war, militia forces supported the colonial army. They continued to use the minuteman model of frequent training and rapid response. The minutemen were irregular troops, which

At the Battles of Lexington and Concord, the minutemen shot at the retreating British soldiers from the cover of trees and rocks.

means they were not part of the regular army. They didn't march and fight in formation, but instead operated as **sharpshooters** (expert marksman who fired from long distances) or **skirmishers** (fighters on the edge of a battle, usually making unplanned smaller attacks of opportunity). They could **harass** the British, hold key points such as bridges, and provide support for the main army. They helped America win its independence from the British.

Paul Revere

One of the most famous minutemen is Paul Revere. A silversmith by profession, Revere was also an avid patriot who wanted the colonies to be free from British rule. He was a member of the Sons of Liberty, the group responsible for the Boston Tea Party, when a cargo of tea was dumped into Boston Harbor to protest British taxation.

Revere is best known for his "Midnight Ride." Along with many other patriots in Boston, Revere began spying on the British, keeping track of their military activities. They knew about the army's secret planned raid of the Concord weapons long before it occurred, but didn't know exactly when it would happen. When spies saw troops gathering, Revere was sent on horseback to warn other militia members in and around Lexington.

He managed to avoid British patrols and deliver his vital message. More than forty other riders took his warning and spread it even farther. By the time the British arrived, the minutemen and other militia members had mustered, ready to fight.

Contrary to legend, Revere did not shout, "The British are coming!" His mission was secret, and everyone took great pains not to let British troops know the militia was ready for them. Besides that, most colonists still considered themselves to be British at that time. They would have been confused by those words. According to Revere himself, his message was, "The Regulars are coming!"

Minuteman Paul Revere warned other patriots that the British Army was on the move.

TWO

What It Took to Be a Minuteman

In the modern United States there is a lot of separation between military and civilian members of society. Members of the armed forces usually work, train, and often live on or near a military base. They don't spend the majority of their time mixing with the general population.

The opposite was true in colonial America. The local armed force (as opposed to the more organized British army) was made up entirely of members of a community. So in every region, the local bakers, silversmiths, farmers, or hunters would be members of the militia. They would live and work at home, and then gather every once in a while for training. The best of these would become the fast-responding minutemen, but even that elite unit lived and worked at home unless they were deployed for an emergency.

Hunting was largely forbidden for the middle and lower classes of England.
Yet in the colonies everyone was allowed to hunt, and many did.

From Hunters to Minutemen

Though they received training, many members of these militias
entered military service with skills that would be useful to them.
Particularly in the early colonial years, life was hard. Settlers
were trying to carve out their own version of civilization from

the wilderness. Men, women, and even children had to work the land and hunt just to survive. Later, as towns developed, and agriculture, livestock breeding, and trade flourished, life was easier, but many people continued to hunt.

Some hunted to supplement their diets or income. In late winter and early springtime, when stored supplies had almost run out and the next year's crops and livestock weren't ready, people often had to return to hunting and fishing to survive.

Others relied on hunting to make a living. The fur trade was extremely profitable in this period. Professional hunters might live in the wilderness and spend months hunting and trapping, then return to town to sell their pelts. Others went about it in a more amateur way. They lived in town and occasionally hunted in the vast wilderness that still covered much of North America. Some of the most valuable pelts came from beavers, otters, bears, ermine, and deer.

Firearms were relatively common, and many young men (and quite a few young women) learned to shoot. This was the most basic early training for a boy who would grow up to become a minuteman. He might also learn to stalk game through the forest. He could learn how to track and how to walk silently. These are skills that would be very useful as a minuteman.

Hunting and Shooting in Colonial America

When English colonists first arrived in North America, most of them had never hunted before. In England, hunting laws were very strict. From the Middle Ages onward, hunting was a pastime for the elite. Noblemen established game preserves. Poachers who illegally shot deer or trapped animals inside the preserves might be fined, imprisoned, mutilated, or worse.

In the colonies, though, it was entirely different. The whole continent was open for hunting. Craftsmen, merchants, farmers, even the poorest people were allowed to hunt. For the first time, anyone could pick up a rifle and shoot a deer. People could spend time in the wilderness and trap rabbits or shoot ducks without fear of penalty. These woodsmen's skills helped make them ideal minutemen.

The Patriotic Spirit

Although common, guns were expensive, and not everyone owned one. A smooth bore **musket**, the kind most frequently used by the colonial militia, could cost a month's wages or more. Plenty of young men who joined the minutemen had never handled a gun before. Militia leaders,

however, had several other requirements in selecting prospective candidates.

The men selected as minutemen had to be young, usually between sixteen and thirty years old, although there were exceptions. They had to be healthy and active enough to excel at their specialized training, and muster at a moment's notice. They had to be able to march long distances, run for cover, and endure the hardships of a long campaign.

More than physical robustness, the minutemen were looking for personality traits, too. They wanted people who were enthusiastic and devoted. Early on in colonial history, that might have been enough. But in the second half of the eighteenth century, when anger toward Britain was increasing, the minutemen looked for members who were actively sympathetic to the patriot cause. They wanted young men who spoke out against English taxes and English rule. Minutemen couldn't feel like English citizens who happened to be in another land. They had to feel wholeheartedly like citizens of the colonies.

Near the outbreak of the American Revolutionary War, minutemen recruited young men who were devoted to the patriot cause.

THREE

The Daily Life of a Minuteman

Minutemen and other members of the militia were required to train at certain intervals. Early in the colonial period, each company had to gather at least four times a year. As hostilities grew near the start of the Revolutionary War, these gatherings increased to monthly, or in some cases several times a month.

The regular training days were almost like a festival. The community might gather to watch the militia drill and march. Afterward, when their training was finished for the day, the militiamen and their families celebrated as if it was a holiday, with feasts, music, and merrymaking.

Weapons

Minutemen and other militia members used a variety of firearms. The most common, for them and for the British troops, was the

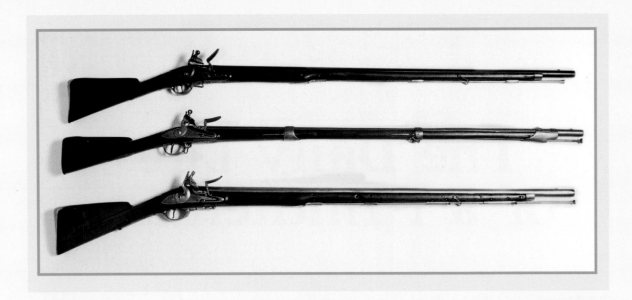

The flintlock musket known as Brown Bess was the most common firearm for minutemen, militia members, and the British Army.

smooth bore flintlock musket, nicknamed Brown Bess. The inside of the barrel of the gun had not been rifled, or cut with spiral grooves to improve the accuracy and range. It was instead smooth like a pipe. The flintlock firing mechanism used a spark from a piece of flint to fire the gun. The Brown Bess had an effective range of about 80 yards (73 meters). It could also be reloaded relatively quickly—in fifteen to twenty seconds.

Another weapon associated with the minutemen is the long rifle. This weapon had many advantages, such as accuracy over long distances. It could be used hundreds of yards away from the enemy to harass them, well out of range of their returning musket fire. The main drawback of these rifles was that they took a long time to reload. The primer, gunpowder, and ball had to be loaded and rammed down separately. A skilled rifleman might still take a minute to reload. So a rifle was excellent for shooting objects that couldn't shoot back, such as deer. When shooting at an army, however, a minuteman often had to retreat after each shot before British troops could move within range. Minutemen thereby became known for their quick hit-and-run

tactics. Fortunately, the long rifle didn't produce as much smoke as the Brown Bess did after each shot. This made it harder for enemy soldiers to pinpoint the exact location from which the rifle shot was fired.

Minutemen might also carry personal firearms, such as dueling pistols. Many carried edged weapons too.

The spiral grooves on the inside of a long rifle barrel made the bullet much more stable over long distances, leading to better accuracy.

Soldiers such as these of the 1st Maryland Regiment used bayonets for close-quarters combat.

Bayonets, or knives that could be attached to the end of a gun without getting in the way of firing, were common. Some also adopted the Native American practice of carrying a small axe called a tomahawk. All of these could be used in close-quarters combat.

Clothing

Unlike the British soldiers in their bright red coats, the minutemen weren't issued special uniforms. They simply wore their own clothing. Although no two minutemen looked the same, there were similarities in their dress.

The typical male suit of the day included a coat, waistcoat (vest), and either breeches (form-fitting pants that fall below the knee and are fastened) or trousers (looser pants that reach shin or ankle length). Lightweight linen shirts worn by hunters in the frontier lands later

No two minutemen dressed exactly alike. They didn't wear uniforms, just their own clothes.

became popular with minutemen. Prior to the Revolutionary War, such shirts were seen as undergarments, and not proper for display.

Three-cornered hats were popular, but so were hats with broad uncocked brims. Wool caps in the cold weather were also common. Shoes might be low with buckles, or laced ankle-length half boots. They were often custom made, but shoes for the left and right foot weren't made differently.

To this was added socks or stockings, a neckerchief, and a greatcoat in cold weather. Of course, any of these might be abandoned depending on weather conditions and the degree of hardship during battle. Most men were clean-shaven, but while on maneuvers they might grow temporary beards. Men's hair was often worn long and tied back in a tight **queue**, a tail tied along the length with ribbon or a leather thong.

Equipment

Minutemen had to always keep their gear ready to respond to any call-out. (Despite the name, they weren't expected to be ready in exactly one minute, but in as short a time as possible, perhaps fifteen to twenty minutes from the first call to being assembled with the other minutemen.) That meant that their knapsack had to always be packed, their gun clean, and their gunpowder

and **ammunition** ready. Minutemen had to strike a balance between having everything they would need on a campaign, and packing light so they could travel swiftly.

The minuteman's knapsack would contain food, a blanket or other bedding, and perhaps a few spare clothes. It would weigh 20 pounds (9.1 kilograms) or more. While modern backpacks for the military or serious hikers have a frame that takes some of the weight off the shoulders and distributes it to the hips,

The minuteman had to have all the equipment he needed to march and fight, but kept his gear light enough to travel quickly.

Sybil Ludington, the "Female Paul Revere"

Though there are no records of female minutemen, there is at least one young girl who is sometimes called the "Female Paul Revere." She too had a famous midnight ride—one that was probably even harder than Revere's.

Sybil Ludington was only sixteen on April 26, 1777, when a message came for her father, a colonel in the New York militia, that the British were attacking a town in nearby Connecticut. Sybil saddled a horse and set out at 9 p.m. She rode 40 miles (64.4 km) through the darkness and heavy rain, alerting her father's four hundred soldiers. Sybil carried a stick, which she used to knock on doors, and also to defend herself from the highwaymen, or robbers, who attacked her. George Washington himself later praised her for her bravery.

Sybil Ludington wasn't a minuteman, but she did a minuteman's job when she rode 40 miles (64.4 kilometers) through the night to muster the militia.

colonial knapsacks placed all the weight on the shoulders. Even 20 pounds (9.1 kg) would feel very heavy after a day of marching.

In addition to the knapsack, minutemen had to carry their ammunition box. It contained enough gunpowder and lead balls used as bullets for at least thirty shots. It would weigh about 10 pounds (4.5 kg). The musket or rifle weighed an additional 10 pounds. Add to that 2 pounds (0.9kg) of water in a canteen, and another pound for a bayonet, and the total weight a minuteman carried was at least 43 pounds (19.5 kg).

Food

While at home, either living with family or participating in periodic training, minutemen ate the same foods as everyone else. On the whole, colonists had a good diet, with more than enough calories and a reasonable balance of the food groups. People also tended to be much more active, offsetting most additional calories.

A typical meal was what was known as a pottage dish, or a stew made from meat simmered with vegetables and grains or cornmeal. It might contain root vegetables such as potatoes, turnips, and carrots, as well as peas, greens, and beans. Beef and pork were often preserved in salt and had to be soaked in water to leech the salt out. Dried corn might have to be boiled for several hours in order to soften. Herbs and spices (other than salt) were rarely used. Meals were generally eaten with bread.

While on campaign, minutemen had to carry much of their food with them. The weekly food ration for Virginia militia members in the field in 1757 included 7 pounds (3.2 kg) of flour and 7 pounds of beef or pork, probably salted and dried. They were able to supplement these provisions with hunting, gathering, or by purchasing fresh food at sympathetic farms.

Drink

Beer, and especially after 1700, hard apple cider, were the beverages of choice. These drinks were good ways to preserve the bounty of wheat (beer) and apples (cider) through the winter. These usually contained much less alcohol than beer or cider today, often less than one percent. Even children would drink beer and cider.

People didn't usually drink water, because it often carried diseases such as typhus, or organisms that caused diarrhea. There was no plumbing, and water was often contaminated by human waste. It was only safe to drink if it had been boiled for tea or coffee (or sometimes if it was from a wilderness source far from human habitation.) Even a small amount of alcohol, however, killed most contaminants.

Travel

Without motorized transportation, travel was fairly slow. Most people traveled by **shank's mare**—meaning by foot.

Some traveled by horseback, which was fastest over short distance. A well-trained cavalry horse in good condition could travel 30–40 miles (48.3–64.4 kilometers) each day. However, a horse could not travel that distance every day. A wagon pulled by mules or horses might cover 15–25 miles (24–40 km) each day. A team of oxen could pull a wagon 10–12 miles (16–19 km) every day. Though slower, oxen don't require as much good food or rest as horses. These distances all assume decent roads and conditions. On hills or in wet weather they would all travel much more slowly.

Minutemen relied on all of these methods for travel. Those who could afford it kept a fast horse for covering short distances very quickly.

FOUR

The Organized Minutemen

In September and October of 1774, the colonies resolved to dramatically improve their militias. They decided to focus on the militia rather than try to create a standing professional army because the British would immediately (and rightly) suspect that the colonials were planning for war. The long-standing tradition of having a militia for defense of the colonies wouldn't arouse as much suspicion. Still, the colonial leaders wanted to do their best to make the militia as close as possible to a regular army by increasing training and provisions.

In October 1774, the First Continental Congress made the minutemen official. The concept of the minuteman had existed since the earliest colonial days. Now, in the months before the American Revolution, colonial leaders saw how vital they might be when open warfare began.

Preparation for War

First, the Congress created a committee of safety, which had the authority to raise the alarm and assemble as much of the militia as they thought was needed. It further created a committee of supply to provision the militia with food and weapons. Prior to that, most militia members had to provide their own supplies, and some did not have everything they needed.

Next, the Congress organized the new militia. It decreed that the regiments should choose their own officers. From each regiment, the officers would select one-quarter of the best militia members and put them into new companies of fifty men each. These men, all privates, would then elect from their ranks one captain and two lieutenants for each company. The newly formed minutemen would "equip and hold themselves in readiness, on the shortest notice from the said committee of safety, to march to the place of rendezvous ..."

Nine companies would join together to form one battalion of 450 men. The officers of each company would elect field officers to command the entire battalion. All of these new elections of officers meant that the anti-British colonists, who were in the majority, could force most of the loyalists (those who supported continued British rule) out of the militia. Now most of the groups were led by seasoned veterans of the French and Indian War, and utterly loyal to the Patriot cause.

The intention had been for the companies to gather to train at the regimental level, in large groups of several battalions. In reality, this was difficult to do because of the distance between companies, and also because it was sometimes hard to pay the troops during longer training sessions. Most of the time, they trained at the local company level.

The British Army

The British Army and the colonial militias were very different. The British army had a very strict hierarchy. Enlisted men could not question the orders of officers, and had very little say in anything. Officers usually came from the wealthiest families and bought their

A British Army officer was usually from a wealthy family and had purchased his commission.

commissions. A commission at that time would cost around £450 ($702.94 in US dollars) or more depending on the rank purchased.

Junior officers couldn't make any decisions themselves. They had to wait for their superiors to issue commands. That meant many valuable opportunities were wasted while riders galloped back and forth with instructions. Even if an officer made a bad decision or gave an order that would lead to disaster, the men under him had to follow his orders or risk being charged with mutiny and executed.

Earned, Not Bought

The minutemen on the other hand, did not purchase their positions—they earned them. The organization was in some ways democratic. The men got to choose their own leaders from among their ranks. They would pick men they had faith in, men whose military skill and instincts they trusted and wanted to follow.

Once deployed, the difference between minutemen and the British army regulars became even more apparent. Minutemen had more freedom than the British army regulars. Companies could act independently of officers above them in the hierarchy. This made sense, because the purpose of the minutemen was to deliver a lightning-fast response to any threat. They couldn't do that if they had to always wait for orders from their higher-ups.

The Mechanics

One of the earliest patriot spy groups was a Boston organization known as the Mechanics, or the Liberty Boys. In that time, a mechanic was any skilled worker, such as a silversmith. Paul Revere was one of the Mechanics. Other minutemen were among their ranks.

In 1774 and 1775, the thirty or so men who formed the Mechanics made a pact to monitor the British, gather intelligence, and do anything they could to sabotage British interests and disrupt the British army. The Mechanics managed to steal some British military equipment in Boston. Working

Silversmith and minuteman Paul Revere was one of the many patriots who spied on the British and worked secretly to liberate the colonies from Britain.

in pairs, they watched every movement the British troops made. By careful observation and with information gathered from their sources, the Mechanics learned in advance about the secret attack the British planned for the supplies at Concord.

Mechanics were successful in this plot. However, the overall operation wasn't always well planned. For example, they always met at the Green Dragon Tavern, making it easier for the British to keep track of them. One of their members was even a British agent spying on them. Despite this, it is probable that the British didn't realize how big the colonial militia was, and thereby underestimated the threat of the Mechanics and other patriots.

Messengers and Spies

Minutemen also developed a very efficient spy and communication system. Because they lived among the population rather than being quartered separately, they could use their family and friends as part of their information network. In fact, many civilians were also effective spies, monitoring British troop movements and listening for whispers of gossip that could tip them off to planned attacks. Later in the American Revolution, the colonial side used such spy

Paul Revere's Midnight Ride was part of a very effective "alarm and muster" system used by the colonial militia.

techniques as invisible ink and secret codes. It is possible that the minutemen did the same.

Fast and efficient communication was absolutely vital to the success of the minutemen. Without telephones, they relied on a system of runners and horsemen to spread the word. Each minuteman had certain other members who he was responsible for notifying as soon as an alarm was called. For example, just before the Battles of Lexington and Concord, Paul Revere was charged with alerting patriots Samuel Adams and John Hancock in Lexington. He told other minutemen along the way, and as they received the warning that the army was advancing, each told the other minutemen on their list, who would tell others, and so on. Soon everyone heard the news.

In addition to riders and runners, towns also used other systems to communicate. Bells, drums, horns, gunshots, and bonfires were all used at various times to deliver messages quickly from town to town.

FIVE

The Minuteman Legacy

Before the outbreak of the American Revolutionary War, the British underestimated the full fighting strength of the minutemen and the colonial militia. They had the impression that they were casual soldiers, poorly trained, and unmotivated. But there were far more minutemen than the British realized, and their tactics and training included not just hit-and-run bush warfare, but conventional battle training, too. They weren't a disorganized rabble, but a large group of skilled soldiers. The minutemen became the core of the new Continental Army.

From Militia to Army

Shortly after Lexington and Concord, the Second Continental Congress resolved to raise an army of 14,600 men. They planned for that number to swell to 30,000 before long. Because of the size of the existing militia, this number was quickly reached. The officers of the minutemen were chief among those selected to lead the new Continental Army regiments. Many of the minutemen privates also chose to join the army. Their experience made them valuable members, but their tactics had to change.

The minutemen and other militia didn't just shoot at people from behind rocks. They also operated in small attack groups that, while

The British Army marched and fought in lines. When militia members joined the Continental Army, they had to learn these tactics.

not as organized as the British Army, did work together successfully. However, when the minutemen moved to the new Continental Army, they had to learn to move and fight in organized lines like the British.

Fighting in a Straight Line

This type of warfare seems strange to many people today. Soldiers would line up opposite each other and fire at their enemy, all the while standing still and being targets themselves. In ranks three men deep, they would continue to fire at each other, and gradually move closer. Finally, when they were near, they would break from their lines and fight in close combat with bayonets.

Using these methods, a battle was won or lost by firing speed. An experienced company could fire and reload about four times a minute. Exceptional units might manage one more shot. If one side could be just a little faster to reload and fire, they would probably win. Accuracy of each shot didn't really matter. Soldiers didn't aim for specific targets, but just shot into the group. The former minutemen had some experience with the marching and drills, but they were usually very skilled at rapid reloading. They adapted well to these techniques.

Even after the creation of the Continental Army, the colonials still employed skirmishers and riflemen to harass the British and engage in small battles beyond the scope of the main maneuvers. And there was still an active militia of reserves to fill the ranks of the army or to defend individual towns if the main colonial military force was far away.

The minutemen and the militia never played as big a role in the Revolutionary War as they did at Lexington and Concord. But the minuteman idea—that each member should be ready to deploy with all his gear at a minute's notice—never vanished, and the colonial military remained more fluid and maneuverable than the British Army.

The Minuteman in Perspective

Changing views of history have put the minutemen in different perspectives. Some of that has to do with **propaganda**, or information (often misleading or inaccurate) used to promote a particular view. At the start of the Revolutionary War, the colonists were looking for allies against Britain. They needed money and supplies from Europe. They also needed to build support at home. So they needed to portray the colonists as suffering victims, and the British as the cruel aggressors.

Early reports of the minutemen's actions at Lexington and Concord didn't show how valiantly they fought. They were often portrayed as hardly firing a shot, and being at the mercy of the attacking British. Even paintings and engravings made around that time show aggressive British firing at helpless minutemen. The patriots went to great lengths to control which facts were released to make sure that Britain took the blame for starting the conflict. This earned the sympathy of other countries such as France and convinced them to support the patriot side.

Later, though, the truth about the fierce resistance of the minutemen emerged. The war was won, America had gained its independence, and citizens were proud of the role the minutemen had played. People finally admitted that the minutemen took an active role in fighting the British, and gave better than they got. Today, the minutemen and the other militia members are recognized for the strength, persistence, and skill of their resistance in the opening salvo of the American Revolutionary War.

The minutemen's role in the Battles of Lexington and Concord won them a place on the Massachusetts state quarter.

Minutemen Pranksters

Most of the British Army looked on the colonial militia as something of a joke. The British Army had practiced the same type of training for generations. It mostly consisted of very long, rigorous marching drills. Huge numbers of men had to learn to move in exact formation following very precise orders.

The colonial militia, however, paid very little attention to marching and drills. In fact the militia themselves made fun of the parade-ground discipline. For example, one of the usual ways for a militia member to salute a commanding officer was to fire a blank charge from his musket into the dirt near that officer's feet. It was considered an accomplishment if he could startle his officer. A British soldier who did that would, at the very least, be court-martialed and whipped.

The British viewed the minutemen and all of the colonial militia as a bunch of undisciplined pranksters. They did not realize that those marching drills were useless for the kind of fighting the minutemen planned to use. They used all that valuable time they saved to practice something much more important: rapid firing and marksmanship—which was evident at Lexington and Concord.

GLOSSARY

ammunition   The bullets, balls, or shells fired from guns, sometimes including the gunpowder, primer, or fuses used to fire them.

bayonet   A blade attached to the muzzle, or firing end, of a firearm.

civilian   A person who is not in the armed forces or law enforcement.

colony   A region under control of another country, often a distant one.

elite   A small part of a larger group that is superior in ability or some quality.

harass   To make small, repeated attacks on an enemy.

Mechanics   A group of approximately thirty patriots who took turns during day and night to watch the movement of British regulars and loyalists in Boston and then met regularly to discuss the collected information.

militia   A military body made up of civilians who can be called in time of need.

minuteman   A member of the American militia in colonial and Revolutionary times who could be ready for action on very short notice.

musket   A lightweight shoulder-fired gun with a smooth bore, loaded from the muzzle end.

muster   To assemble troops for battle.

patriot   A person who supports his or her nation and is prepared to defend it; in the Revolutionary War, a colonist who supported an independent America free from British rule.

propaganda   Information, often misleading or incorrect, used to deliberately sway a person's opinions.

queue   In hairstyles, a pigtail gathered tightly and wound with ribbon or leather.

rifle   A long gun with spiral grooves cut into its barrel to give the bullet spin for better accuracy over long distances.

salvo	A period when weapons are fired at the same time; a sudden attack.
shank's mare	Slang for walking, based on the idea that a person's shanks, or legs, are their horse.
sharpshooter	A person capable of making highly accurate shots with a firearm.
silversmith	A craftsman skilled in the manipulation of silver into jewelry or other articles.
skirmisher	One who participates in irregular, often spontaneous or unplanned fighting, especially along the edges of a battle.
taxation	Mandatory contribution to the government's revenue, generally as a percentage of income or the value of goods.

Find Out More

BOOKS

Ellis, Carol. *The Military in Colonial America*. Life in Colonial America. New York: Cavendish Square, 2014.

Raum, Elizabeth. *The Dreadful, Smelly Colonies: The Disgusting Details About Life in Colonial America*. Minneapolis, MN: Capstone Press, 2011.

Schanzer, Rosalyn. *George vs. George: The American Revolution as Seen from Both Sides*. Des Moines, IA: National Geographic Children's Books, 2007.

WEBSITES

America's Story

www.americaslibrary.gov/jb/colonial/jb_colonial_subj.html

Discover more moments in American history through this site from the Library of Congress. Read articles written for kids and explore a large section titled Colonial America, and another called the Revolutionary Period.

US History.org: Minutemen

www.ushistory.org/people/minutemen.htm

This website offers a brief history of the minutemen and colonial militias during the American Revolution, including their history, background, battles, and impact on the war.

MUSEUMS

Colonial Williamsburg

www.history.org

This living history museum in Williamsburg, Virginia, recreates an entire colonial city. The 301-acre (121.8-hectare) site has many original historic buildings and actor/docents who reenact colonial life. The website is also full of valuable information about the era.

Minute Man National Historical Park

www.nps.gov/mima/index.htm

This 970-acre (392.5 ha) park in and around the towns of Lincoln, Lexington, and Concord, Massachusetts, has several prominent sites that relate to minutemen and the Battles of Lexington and Concord, including the Lexington Battle Green and a historic trail that approximates the route of the running battle.

Index

Page numbers in **boldface** are illustrations. Entries in **boldface** are glossary terms.

About the Author

Laura L. Sullivan is the author of many fiction and nonfiction books for children, including the fantasy *Under the Green Hill* and the romance *Love by the Morning Star*. She has also co-written an upcoming romantic mystery set in the Golden Age of Hollywood, with famed director and producer Adam Shankman. She is the author of many books for Cavendish Square, including six titles in the Colonial People series.